I ♥ *my* **lady business**

Cindy Borgatti

Cindy Borgatti (signature)

I ♥
my **lady**
business

Cindy Borgatti, Body Sugarist

Friendly and down to earth are just two ways to describe me. I use a no-nonsense and most times humorous approach in putting hundreds of ladies at ease during a full Brazilian sugaring service. My goal is to make every client feel comfortable, at ease and of course smooth.

Stay smooth and ditch the razor!

conclusion

While "'vagina" is clinically the correct term, it still sparks an embarrassed blush to bashful peoples cheeks. Thus, it has given rise to many variations of the term, some deemed more polite and appropriate for mixed company and some just downright strange. I don't believe there is a right or wrong name. It's what you feel comfortable with and that's all that really matters in my line of "Lady Business".

cooch(ie)

Is it just me, or is this not what we say to babies – "coochie coochie coo."

clam

If you think about it for a minute it'll become more and more obvious.

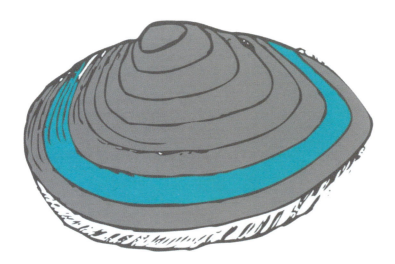

kitty

It's safe to say that this term is self-explanatory. *Am I right ladies?*

fanny

In British slang, ones fanny refers to ones vagina.

biscuit

You know you're redneck when it's called a biscuit.

box

Certainly not the most flattering name,
but it is what it is.

chia pet

In reference to when the yard is
a tad over-grown.

foo foo

Can you say high
maintenance!?!

lady business

Classy and stylish. Ladies take care of business and their lady business.

bird

A popular saying, clients leave de-feathered and singing.

70's fro

Slang used when a client comes in and says,
"It's been awhile since I've been here." Really?!?

cupcake

A work of art to satisfy the sweet tooth.

the frontyard

A beautiful front yard is the ultimate
welcome mat but don't forget
the backyard!

ying yang

Incredibly zen
but this one is
lost on me.

peach

The connection with
food befuddles me,
but I suppose
to some it
makes sense.

vajayjay

A universal word in popular culture due to its use heard on television shows ranging originating on Grey's Anatomy and spreading all the way up to Oprah Winfrey.

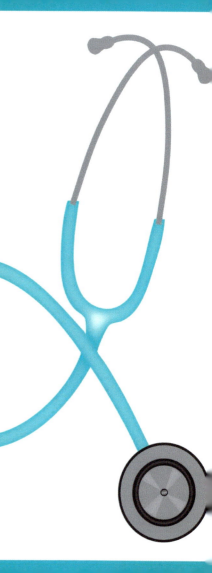

vag

Straight up and to the point. A term more than likely used by a no nonsense kind of person. It has a good ring to it, no?

muffin

No longer just a term used to describe our love handles, though we may not look at a muffin the same way ever again.

beaver

An oldie but goodie. It's a classic reference that never dies.

I love that I have a natural gift of making people laugh during an otherwise incredibly awkward situation and that I can turn it into a quick and fun experience for my client. An added bonus is the bond that develops and leads to some very interesting conversations. It is through those conversations (and much laughter) that the idea to write this book was born. I've come across many different names a lady uses when referring to, for lack of a better term, her lady business, and this book is a collaboration of names used by my clients to celebrate our private parts. When providing such a personal service one must have a sense of humour. I hope upon reading this book you'll get a glimpse into the laughter that comes from my sugar room and perhaps share a laugh yourself.

-- *Cindy Borgatti*

an endless fascination

exists around the mystery that is hair removal, especially the Brazilian, and the idea that I spend more time in other lady's nether regions than most ob-gyns is a never-ending topic of conversation. Whether it is spin class, weddings or dinner parties, the "Lady Business" subject always seems to come up. I consider what I do to be as natural as ordering a cup of coffee. Though I suppose comparing a Starbucks barista's technique in slinging lattes to ripping hair from ones most intimate areas might seem a little far-fetched, I wouldn't do anything else.

dedication

To my clients for making me laugh every day.

To my family for putting up with my face in technology 24/7.

To my friends and co-workers who keep me strong and my spirits up.

I love you all.

-- Cindy Borgatti

Creative: Scott Newlands Creative - scottnewlands.com
Publisher: New Author Publishing - newauthorpublishing.com
Visit us at www.myladybusiness.ca

to _____

from _____

25689013R10019

Made in the USA
Charleston, SC
09 January 2014